105 Writing Prompts for Kids: 1st Grade

Would you rather be a pirate or a jungle explorer?
Why?

Who is the best cartoon character? Why?

Would you rather be really tall or really small?

Write about your last Christmas vacation. What did you do?

What is your favorite thing to do in the snow?

Would you rather ride a giraffe or an elephant?

What's the first thing you do when you wake up?

Write about a trip your family took. Where did you go?

Formatted: Centered

Write about a time when you made a new friend.

How did you meet him or her?

Write about your favorite toy. What do you like best about it?

Write about your favorite toy. What do you like best about it?

Write a story about your favorite place in the world.

Why is it so special?

Tell me about a time when you had to be very brave.

If we all lived in the sea, what would our houses look like?

Describe the funniest set of clothes you could imagine anyone wearing!

Write about why it is good to have friends.

What ten toppings would you put on your crazy pizza!

If fruits had personality, what do you think a banana would be like?

What would the world be like if we had a purple sky and orange grass?

What do you do when one of your friends is sad?

If you could be a dessert, what would you be? Why?

Write about an animal that lives in your neighborhood (your pet, a neighbor's pet, or a squirrel or bird who hangs out in your tree). What does the animal like to do?

Write about a time when you learned a new skill.

Did you struggle to learn it at first?

Write about a time when you were bored. What did you do?

Write a story about something special you did with your mom. What did you do?

Tell me about a time when you could smell

something really horrible!

Would your mother let you have a pet dragon? If not, where would you hide it?

Should you be able to study wizardry at school?

What is the most interesting thing you study at school?

Describe why you like your favorite teacher.

Pretend your favorite teddy could talk. What would you ask him or her and what might they say?

If you had a secret superhero name, what would it be? Why?

What is best part of the day? Why?

What is something special you do with your grandparents? How do they make you feel?

Who is the nicest person you know? What makes

him or her so special?

If you could have any pet, what would you have and why? Where would it sleep?

Imagine a lion who wanted to live in the sea? What would the other sea creatures think about that!?

What time is your bedtime? Is this fair?

A princess woke one morning to find she had grown a long, grey beard. Describe what happened next.

What do you want to be when you grow up?

You have the magical power to breathe

underwater! What do you do first?

If you could be on any TV show, what would it be, and why?

Would you rather explore the moon or the ocean?

Why?

Do you like bugs? Why or why not?

What is your favorite movie? Why do you like it?

What gift do you want to receive on your birthday?

What do you love to do with the fallen leaves in your yard?

My favorite ice cream flavor is _____ because _____. (Complete the sentence)

What do you like to do in a rainy day?

What scary character do you want to be on Halloween?

What is your favorite Thanksgiving food?

Make your own monster. Describe him from his toes to his head.

What is the most interesting thing you study at school?

Imagine what cats dream about.

What would you do if your parents told you that

you were going to move?

Last year on Halloween, I was __________ because

____________.

What do you like to do when it gets warm outside?

How do you feel when you do well on a quiz?

Write a story about a secret backyard fortress.

Do you want to have an older brother/sister or a baby brother/sister? Why or why not?

Write about a time when you were upset about something that happened at school. What did you do?

If you could travel to space, what would you want to see?

Write something nice about your best friend. Explain what you like about him or her and what you like to do together.

Imagine what cats dream about.

Invent three really yucky flavors of ice-cream.

What makes you really, really laugh?

If you have a pet unicorn, what will you name him?

Will you ride on his back?

Write about your favorite toy. What do you like best about it?

Which one would you love to have – a remote controlled airplane, boat or car?

Do you love playing outside or just playing with the computer?

What shape and color of a balloon do you want to have?

If you have a bucket of candies from the Halloween,

will you share some to your friends?

What do you love about Easter egg hunting?

If you caught Santa Claus leaving a present for you,

what will you tell him?

What do you think Santa does during the summer?

If you have to ask Santa a gift for Christmas, what

would that be?

What do you want to be when you grow up?

Which one do you like – an Ice Castle or a Stone Castle?

Do you love going to the doctor?

What do you love eating for breakfast?

If you eat breakfast, what kind of drink do you love to drink? Milk, juice or chocolate drink?

What flavor of cupcake do you love to eat?

What flavor of cupcake do you love to eat?

What gift do you want to ask Mom and Dad for your birthday?

I want to give Mom a _____ as a gift on her birthday.

If I make a snowman, I will name him ______.

My favorite chocolate is _____ because ____.

My bestfriend is _________. I like her/him because

_________.

What do you love doing at the beach?

Which one do you like better? The beach or the pool?

I am scared of _____.

Who is faster? The turtle or the bunny?

Which one do you love – hotdogs or burgers?

Can you draw a butterfly? What colors will your butterfly be?

My birth month is _______. I will be ___ years old.

What is your favorite animal from the zoo?

If you are to invent something, what will it be?

What pet do you have at home?

What time do you do your homework?

What games do you love playing in the snow?

Who helps you with your Math homework?

What kind of toys do you have at home?

If you have a treasure chest, what treasures will you hide inside it?

I love my family because _______.